U.S.A. TRAVEL GUIDES

KANSAS

BY ANN HEINRICHS • ILLUSTRATED BY MATT KANIA

The Child's World®
childsworld.com

Published by The Child's World®
1980 Lookout Drive • Mankato, MN 56003-1705
800-599-READ • www.childsworld.com

Photo Credits
Photographs ©: Tommy Brison/Shutterstock Images, cover, 1; Lane Pearman CC2.0, 7; Keneva Photography/Shutterstock Images, 8; Miguel Vieira CC2.0, 11; Shutterstock Images, 12, 24, 35, 38 (top); Frank A. Rinehart/Boston Public Library, 14; Jim Bowen CC2.0, 16; Everett Historical/Shutterstock Images, 19, 21; iStockphoto, 20; Sean F. Boggs/iStockphoto, 23; Dave Newman/Shutterstock Images, 27; Ivan Cholakov/Shutterstock Images, 28; David Ross/Shutterstock Images, 29; m01229 CC2.0, 31; Robin Myerscough CC2.0, 32; Lukasz Stefanski/Shutterstock Images, 38 (bottom)

ISBN 9781503819566
LCCN 2016961132

Printing
Printed in the United States of America
PA02334

Ann Heinrichs is the author of more than 100 books for children and young adults. She has also enjoyed successful careers as a children's book editor and an advertising copywriter. Ann grew up in Fort Smith, Arkansas, and lives in Chicago, Illinois.

About the Author
Ann Heinrichs

Matt Kania loves maps and, as a kid, dreamed of making them. In school he studied geography and cartography, and today he makes maps for a living. Matt's favorite thing about drawing maps is learning about the places they represent. Many of the maps he has created can be found in books, magazines, videos, Web sites, and public places.

About the
Map Illustrator
Matt Kania

On the cover: Fields of sunflowers grow in Kansas.

OUR KANSAS TRIP

KANSAS

L et's take a trip through Kansas! You'll find lots to see and do there. You'll meet Wyatt Earp, gunfighters, and outlaws. You'll pet a bug and fly a plane. You'll spot dinosaurs and prairie dogs. And you'll even see a fish inside a fish.

Does this sound like your kind of fun? Then hop in and buckle up tight. Let's hit the road!

WELCOME TO
KANSAS

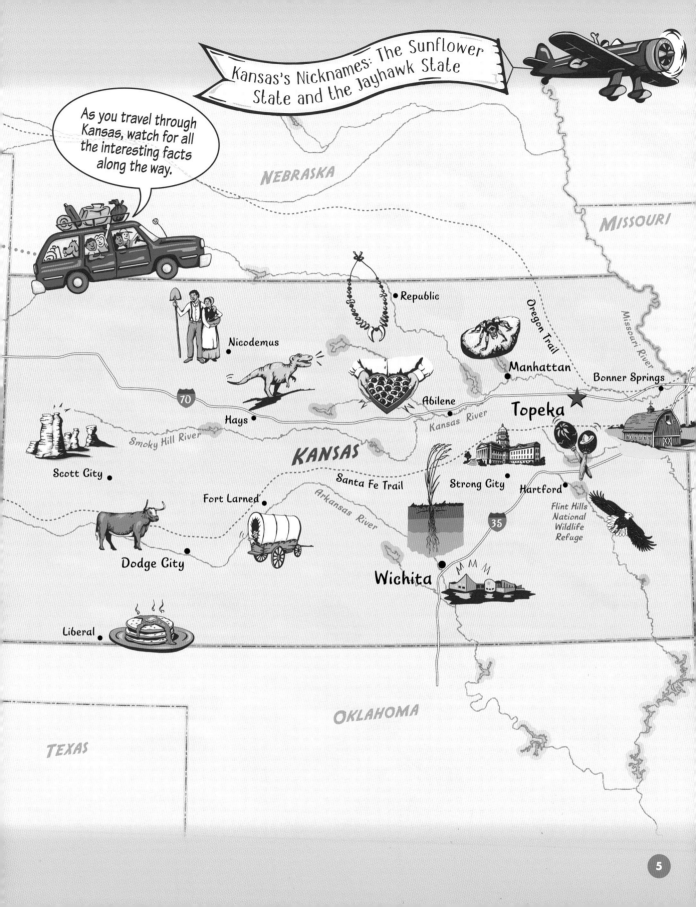

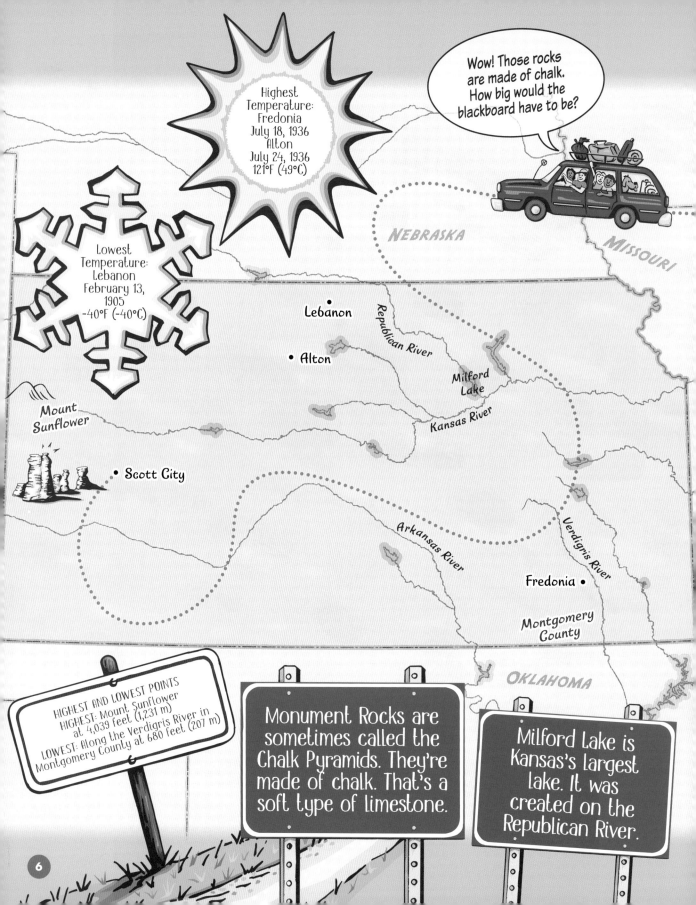

Highest Temperature:
Fredonia July 18, 1936
Alton July 24, 1936
121°F (49°C)

Wow! Those rocks are made of chalk. How big would the blackboard have to be?

Lowest Temperature:
Lebanon February 13, 1905
-40°F (-40°C)

NEBRASKA

MISSOURI

Lebanon

Republican River

Alton

Milford Lake

Mount Sunflower

Kansas River

Scott City

Arkansas River

Verdigris River

Fredonia

Montgomery County

OKLAHOMA

HIGHEST AND LOWEST POINTS
HIGHEST: Mount Sunflower at 4,039 feet (1,231 m)
LOWEST: Along the Verdigris River in Montgomery County at 680 feet (207 m)

Monument Rocks are sometimes called the Chalk Pyramids. They're made of chalk. That's a soft type of limestone.

Milford Lake is Kansas's largest lake. It was created on the Republican River.

The rocks tower high overhead. Some are as tall as seven-story buildings. Some have big holes. You can walk through these holes. It's almost as if they were doors!

You're wandering around Monument Rocks near Scott City. A sea once covered this part of Kansas. Now, high cliffs and strange rocks stand there.

Plains cover most of Kansas. Some are gently rolling plains. Others are just plain flat!

The Arkansas and Kansas rivers run through Kansas. Many smaller rivers flow into them. Kansas has lots of lakes, too. Most were made by building dams on rivers. Water backs up behind a dam. That creates a lake.

See strange, towering rocks at Monument Rocks!

FLINT HILLS NATIONAL WILDLIFE REFUGE

A deer peeks around a tree. Wild turkeys waddle through the grass. Doves are cooing, and ducks are quacking. An eagle soars overhead. You're enjoying a day with nature!

This is Flint Hills National Wildlife Refuge. It's near Hartford in southeastern Kansas. It protects thousands of wild animals.

Kansas's grasslands are home to many animals. You'll find rabbits, raccoons, and coyotes there. And you'll see foxes, weasels, and skunks.

Prairie dogs dig tunnels for homes. Groups of them live together in towns. They have to watch out for snakes. And so do you!

Wild turkeys and many other animals call Flint Hills home.

STATE FLOWER
SUNFLOWER

STATE TREE
COTTONWOOD

STATE BIRD
WESTERN MEADOWLARK

NEBRASKA

MISSOURI

There's a hawk! There's a swan! There's a kite! A kite? Sure. It's a kind of bird.

• Hartford

Flint Hills National Wildlife Refuge

OKLAHOMA

TEXAS

The National Park Service has ten sites in Kansas.

Huge herds of buffalo used to roam across Kansas. Hunters killed almost all of them. Now there are small, protected herds.

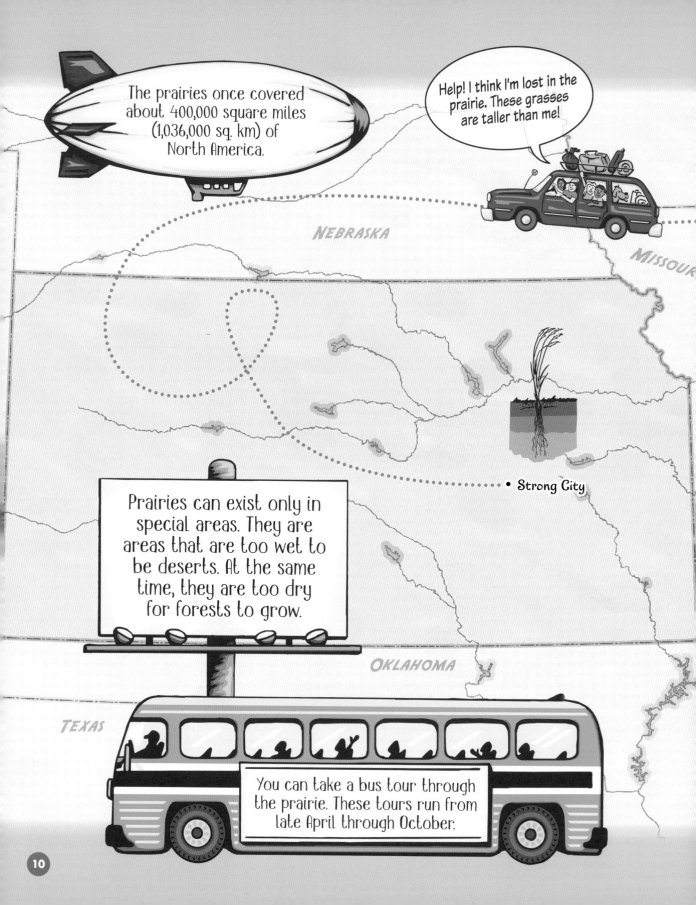

The prairies once covered about 400,000 square miles (1,036,000 sq. km) of North America.

Help! I think I'm lost in the prairie. These grasses are taller than me!

NEBRASKA

MISSOURI

• Strong City

Prairies can exist only in special areas. They are areas that are too wet to be deserts. At the same time, they are too dry for forests to grow.

OKLAHOMA

TEXAS

You can take a bus tour through the prairie. These tours run from late April through October.

TALLGRASS PRAIRIE NATIONAL PRESERVE

Tall grasses once waved across the nation's plains. These grasslands are called tallgrass prairies. They were like a sea of grass. They covered much of the central United States.

Farmers plowed up most of that grass. Only a tiny bit of tallgrass prairie remains. Much of it is in Tallgrass Prairie National Preserve. It's near Strong City.

The preserve's tall grasses could be taller than you. But there are short grasses, too. Many colorful prairie flowers also bloom there.

Coyotes, foxes, and deer live in the preserve. Little mice scurry among the grasses. One is the meadow jumping mouse. It's very tiny. And it jumps!

Don't get lost in the tall grass! Only a small amount of tallgrass prairie is left in Kansas.

THE STERNBERG MUSEUM IN HAYS

Y ou'll love the Sternberg Museum of Natural History in Hays. The fun begins when you walk in. You're face-to-face with a mammoth skeleton! Mammoths were a lot like elephants. They roamed the Earth thousands of years ago.

Don't forget to visit the walkthrough exhibits. They're full of life-size model dinosaurs. You'll be glad they're not alive. Their sharp teeth look ready to bite!

You've got to see the famous fish-within-a-fish. It's the **fossil** skeleton of a huge fish. Inside it is a smaller fish. The big fish ate the little fish. Then the big fish died!

Skeletons of ancient mammoths show they were as big as elephants.

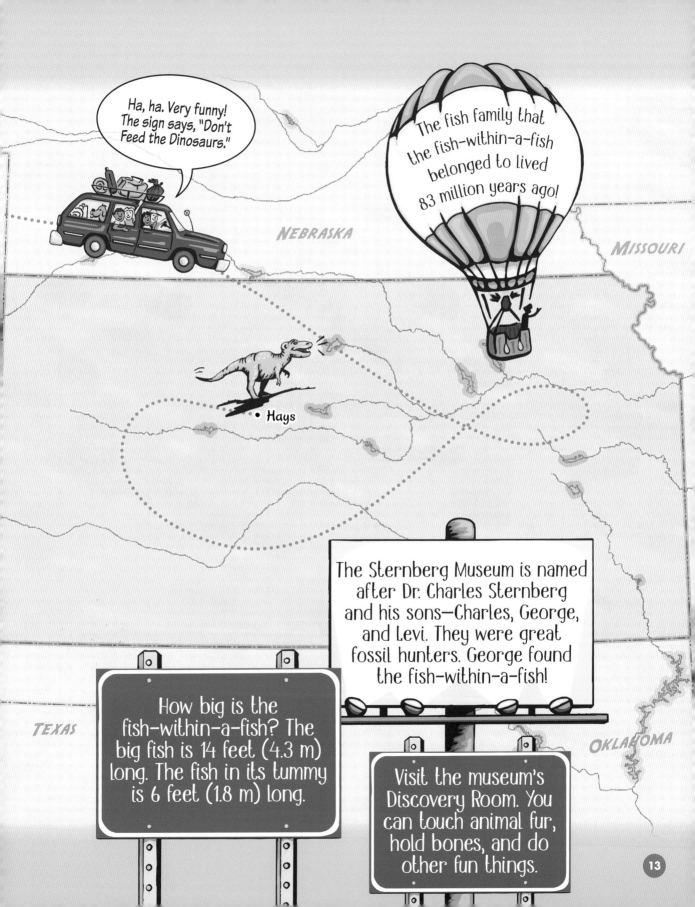

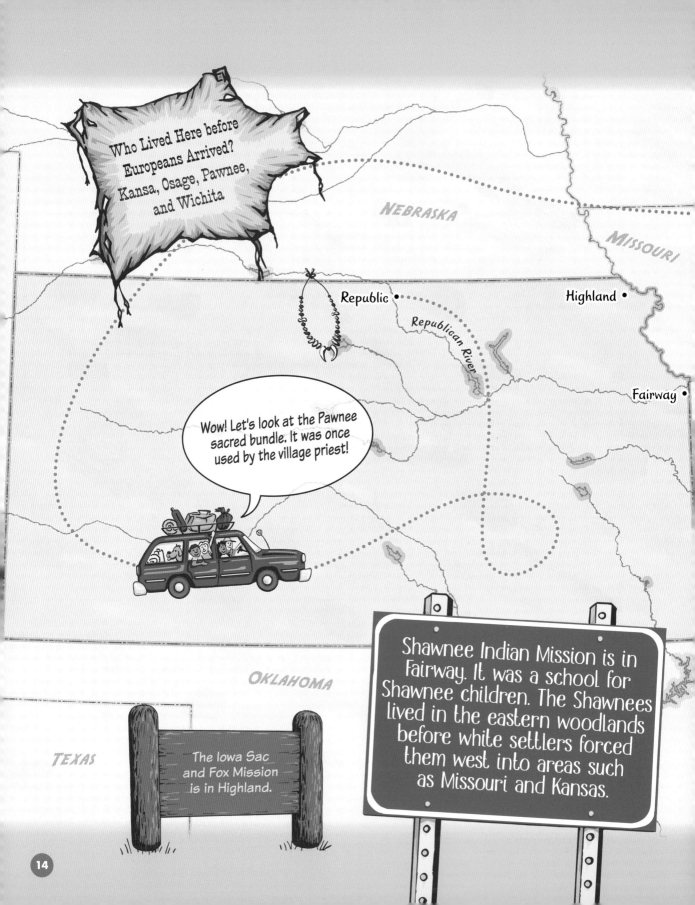

Who Lived Here before Europeans Arrived? Kansa, Osage, Pawnee, and Wichita

NEBRASKA

MISSOURI

Republic •

Republican River

Highland •

Fairway •

Wow! Let's look at the Pawnee sacred bundle. It was once used by the village priest!

OKLAHOMA

TEXAS

The Iowa Sac and Fox Mission is in Highland.

Shawnee Indian Mission is in Fairway. It was a school for Shawnee children. The Shawnees lived in the eastern woodlands before white settlers forced them west into areas such as Missouri and Kansas.

PAWNEE INDIAN MUSEUM

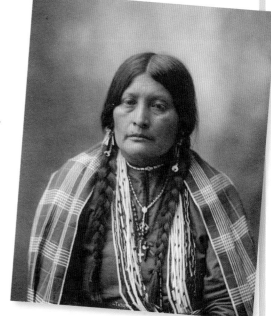

Want to see how Kansas Native Americans once lived? Then head to the Pawnee Indian Museum near Republic! This historical state site has preserved a large Pawnee village.

About 1,000 Pawnee Native Americans lived at this site along the Republican River in 1820. However, the Pawnee left the village and moved north once the land became infertile.

Years later, archaeologists found the remains of 22 Pawnee lodges and 40 storage pits. Visitors can walk the floor of a Pawnee lodge, view a star chart painted on animal skin, inspect items made from the bones of buffalo, and look at Pawnee paintings.

Many Native American tribes still live in Kansas today. They are the Arapaho, Comanche, Cheyenne, Kansa, Osage, Kiowa, Wichita, and Pawnee tribes.

Wichita Native Americans have lived in Kansas since before Europeans arrived.

The soldiers look like they're from the 1850s. They line up and march with their guns. Then, pow! They fire into the air. It's Santa Fe Trail Days at Fort Larned!

Fort Larned was one of many army forts in Kansas. Some forts protected traders and their goods in Kansas. Traders used Fort Larned when traveling on the Santa Fe Trail.

Others forts were used to protect **pioneers**. The pioneers were heading west. Some used the Oregon Trail. That trail went through northeast Kansas. The pioneers hoped to settle in a new place.

Pioneer families and traders traveled in covered wagons. The wagon wheels left deep ruts, or ditches. You can still see those ruts today!

Fort Larned has many historic buildings for visitors to see.

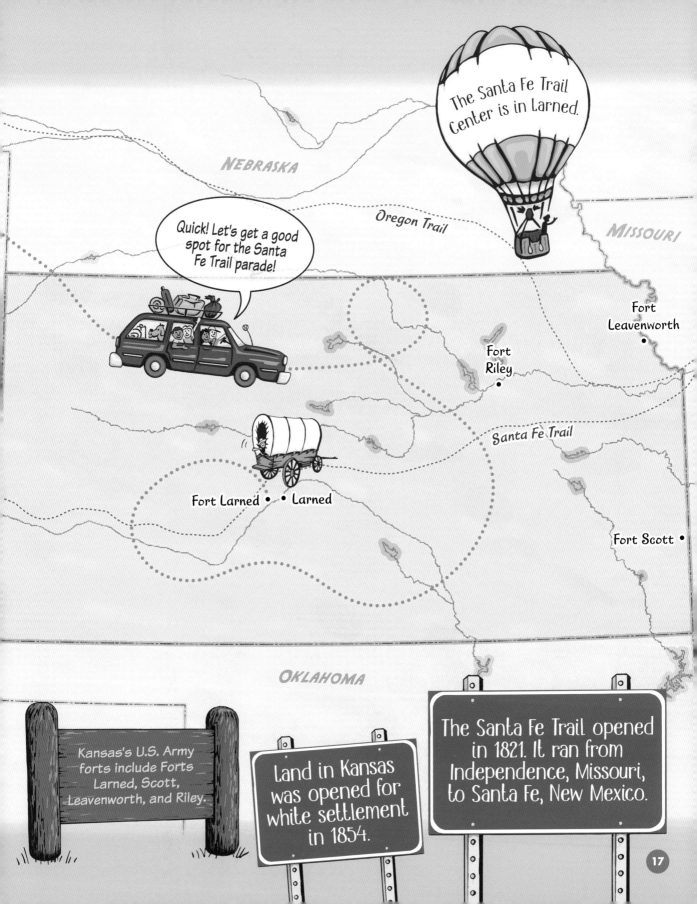

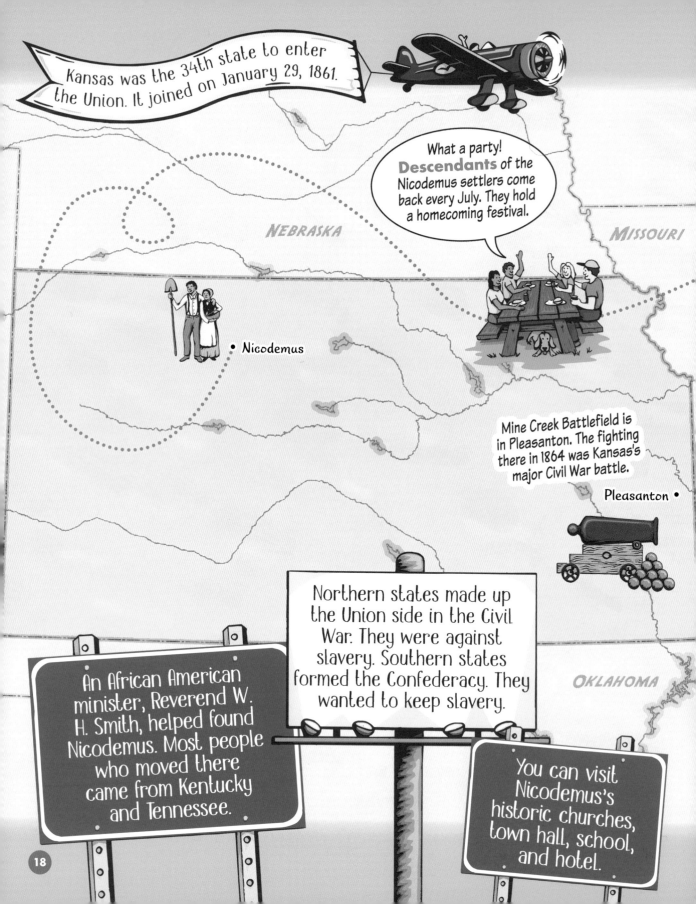

Kansas was the 34th state to enter the Union. It joined on January 29, 1861.

What a party! **Descendants** of the Nicodemus settlers come back every July. They hold a homecoming festival.

NEBRASKA

MISSOURI

• Nicodemus

Mine Creek Battlefield is in Pleasanton. The fighting there in 1864 was Kansas's major Civil War battle.

Pleasanton •

Northern states made up the Union side in the Civil War. They were against slavery. Southern states formed the Confederacy. They wanted to keep slavery.

OKLAHOMA

An African American minister, Reverend W. H. Smith, helped found Nicodemus. Most people who moved there came from Kentucky and Tennessee.

You can visit Nicodemus's historic churches, town hall, school, and hotel.

NICODEMUS, BLEEDING KANSAS, AND THE CIVIL WAR

Nicodemus is a special town. African American people founded it in 1877. Before that, Northern and Southern states argued about slavery. Both sides wanted more states to agree with their view. Things got violent in the 1850s. Kansas was just about to become a state.

People from both sides came into Kansas. They tried to force their views on everyone. Some people were killed as they fought. Kansas got the nickname Bleeding Kansas.

Finally, the Civil War (1861–1865) broke out. The North won, and slavery ended. Many former slaves had nowhere to go. That's why an African American minister founded Nicodemus. He invited former slaves to join him there. The population grew until 1910, when around 400 people lived there.

Nicodemus is a town that some African American people lived in after the Civil War.

DODGE CITY AND BOOT HILL

Watch the gunfighters shoot it out. Try some mechanical bull riding. It's time for Dodge City Days! This summer festival celebrates Dodge City's cowboy past.

Cowboys drove their cattle to Kansas in the 1870s. The cattle were shipped out on railroad cars. Dodge City, Abilene, and Wichita were railroad centers. They were called cowtowns.

Cowboys got pretty wild in the cowtowns. Lawmen tried to keep the peace. Of course, some outlaws got shot. Many ended up in Boot Hill Cemetery in Dodge City.

Stop by Dodge City's Boot Hill Museum. You'll learn all about the cowboy days. You'll see the saloon and other old buildings. And you might even see a gunfight!

At Boot Hill Museum, you'll see old buildings from the cowboy days!

THE AG CENTER IN BONNER SPRINGS

Choo choo! All aboard! You're riding a train around Farm Town USA. This town is part of a huge farm museum in Bonner Springs called the National Agricultural Center and Hall of Fame. People call it the Ag Center for short.

Farming has always been important in Kansas. Millions of beef cattle graze on the plains. Golden fields of wheat stretch across the plains, too. Mills grind that wheat into flour. Kansas is one of the top wheat producing states.

Farming is an important industry in Kansas.

TOPEKA'S FIESTA MEXICANA

Do you like hot food? Then stop by Topeka's Fiesta Mexicana. It's a five-day **Hispanic** festival in July. You'll eat tacos and other Mexican foods. You can even dance to a mariachi band. And here's the hot part. You can enter the **jalapeño**-eating contest. Those peppers will set your mouth on fire!

Hispanic people are one of Kansas's several **ethnic** groups. People from Germany and Sweden were early settlers. Many groups arrived in the early 1900s. They included Italians, Mexicans, and Croatians. Each group brought its native foods and customs.

Don't forget to listen to the mariachi band at Fiesta Mexicana!

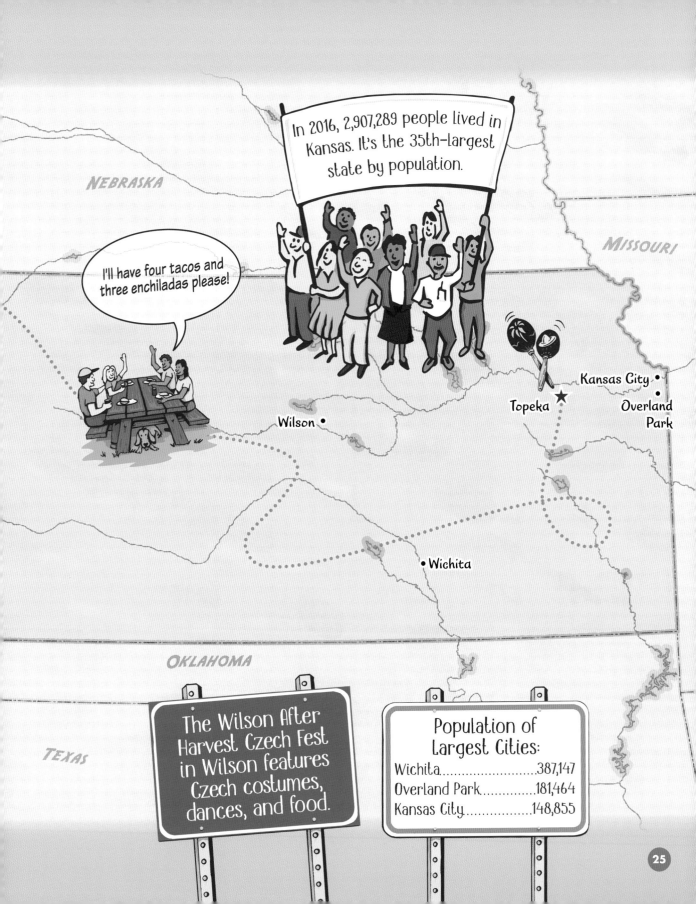

In 2016, 2,907,289 people lived in Kansas. It's the 35th-largest state by population.

I'll have four tacos and three enchiladas please!

Wilson

Topeka

Kansas City

Overland Park

Wichita

The Wilson After Harvest Czech Fest in Wilson features Czech costumes, dances, and food.

Population of Largest Cities:
Wichita........................387,147
Overland Park.............181,464
Kansas City................148,855

THE STATE CAPITOL IN TOPEKA

The capitol in Topeka is full of history lessons. But you don't need to read them. Just look at them! The capitol has huge murals, or wall paintings. They show famous events in Kansas's history.

Kansas's state government offices are in the capitol. There are three branches of state government. One branch makes the laws. Another branch carries out the laws. The governor heads this branch. Judges make up the third branch. The judges meet in courts. They decide whether laws have been broken.

Lawmakers are hard at work in the state capitol building.

Make your own airplane. Then test it in a wind tunnel. Now hop into an airplane pilot's seat. You'll see what it's like to fly over Kansas!

You're at Wichita's Exploration Place. It's a great science center. One section explores airplanes and flying. Just walk in and take the controls!

Airplanes are a big deal in Kansas. During World War II (1939–1945), Kansas factories built many airplanes. The U.S. government used the airplanes in the war.

Airplanes became a big industry in the state. Today, Wichita is Kansas's major aircraft center.

Many World War II airplanes were made in Kansas.

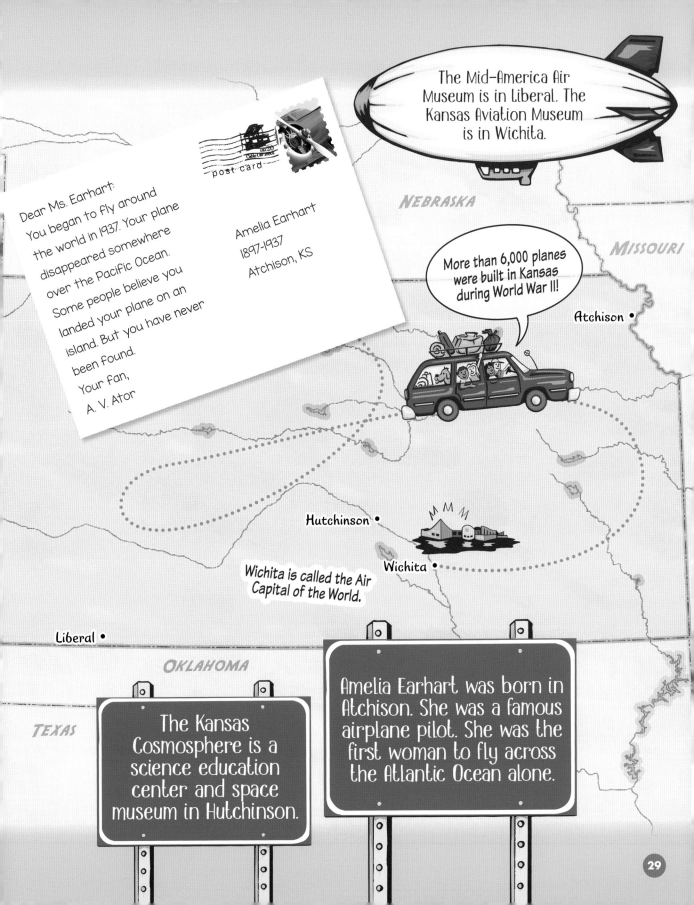

The Mid-America Air Museum is in Liberal. The Kansas Aviation Museum is in Wichita.

Dear Ms. Earhart:
You began to fly around the world in 1937. Your plane disappeared somewhere over the Pacific Ocean. Some people believe you landed your plane on an island. But you have never been found.
Your fan,
A. V. Ator

Amelia Earhart
1897-1937
Atchison, KS

post card

NEBRASKA

MISSOURI

More than 6,000 planes were built in Kansas during World War II!

Atchison •

Hutchinson •

Wichita •

Wichita is called the Air Capital of the World.

Liberal •

OKLAHOMA

TEXAS

The Kansas Cosmosphere is a science education center and space museum in Hutchinson.

Amelia Earhart was born in Atchison. She was a famous airplane pilot. She was the first woman to fly across the Atlantic Ocean alone.

29

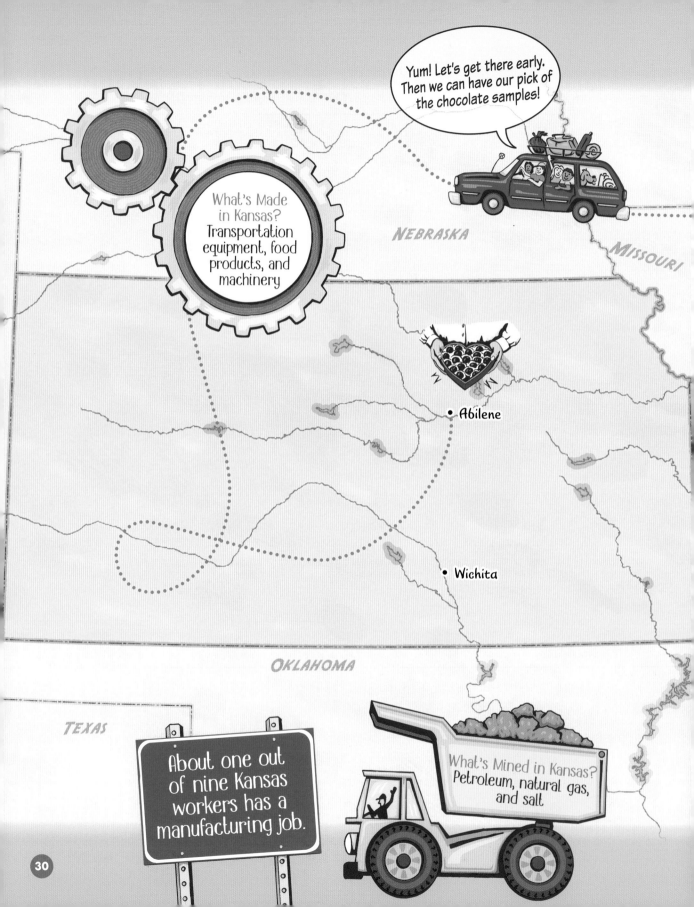

RUSSELL STOVER CANDIES IN ABILENE

Can you smell the chocolate? Then you're getting close to Russell Stover Candies in Abilene. Come inside and take a tour. You'll see the candy cooks at work. And you'll get to eat some samples, too!

Candy is one of Kansas's many food products. Other factories make flour or animal food. Some food plants prepare beef for sale.

Airplanes are one of the state's leading factory goods. There are many airplane factories around Wichita. Some make military airplanes for the U.S. government. Others make small planes for private use. Kansas also makes parts for airplanes, trains, and cars.

Like chocolate? Then tour Russell Stover Candies!

RACING WITH PANCAKES IN LIBERAL

Women are racing down the street. Each one is carrying a skillet. They're flipping pancakes while they run!

You're watching the **International** Pancake Race in Liberal. Why is it international? Because women are also racing in Olney, England. Pancake flippers race in both towns at once!

Kansas has lots of fun events. Many cities have rodeos or Wild West festivals. Some events celebrate pioneer days.

There are several places to enjoy nature. Some people like watching birds in wildlife areas. Others enjoy hiking or horseback riding. The state's many lakes are popular, too. People use them for boating, swimming, and fishing.

Women in Olney, England, participate in the International Pancake Race.

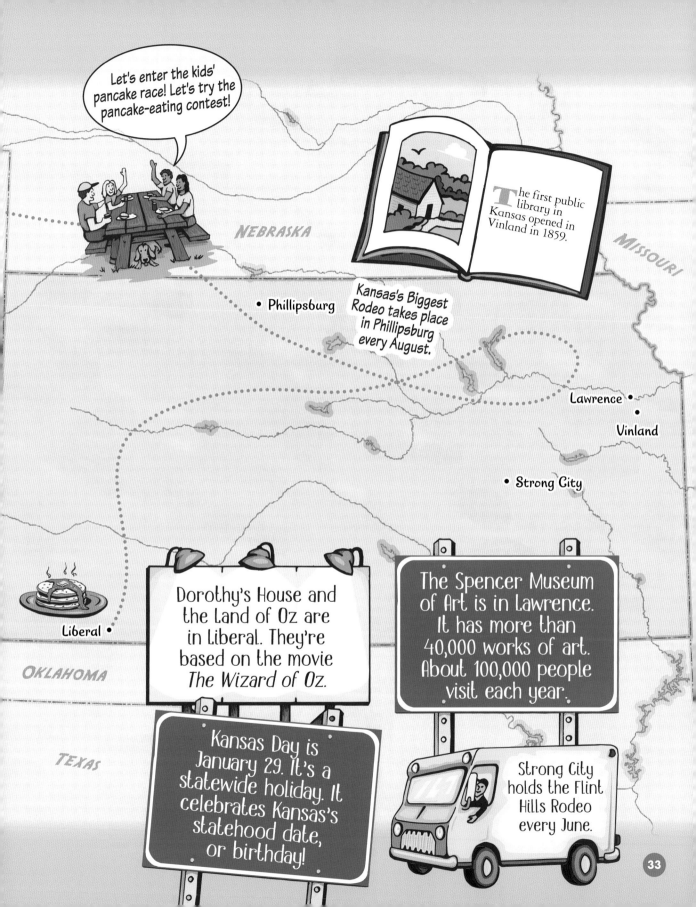

Let's enter the kids' pancake race! Let's try the pancake-eating contest!

NEBRASKA

MISSOURI

The first public library in Kansas opened in Vinland in 1859.

• Phillipsburg

Kansas's Biggest Rodeo takes place in Phillipsburg every August.

Lawrence •

Vinland •

• Strong City

Dorothy's House and the Land of Oz are in Liberal. They're based on the movie *The Wizard of Oz*.

The Spencer Museum of Art is in Lawrence. It has more than 40,000 works of art. About 100,000 people visit each year.

Liberal •

OKLAHOMA

TEXAS

Kansas Day is January 29. It's a statewide holiday. It celebrates Kansas's statehood date, or birthday!

Strong City holds the Flint Hills Rodeo every June.

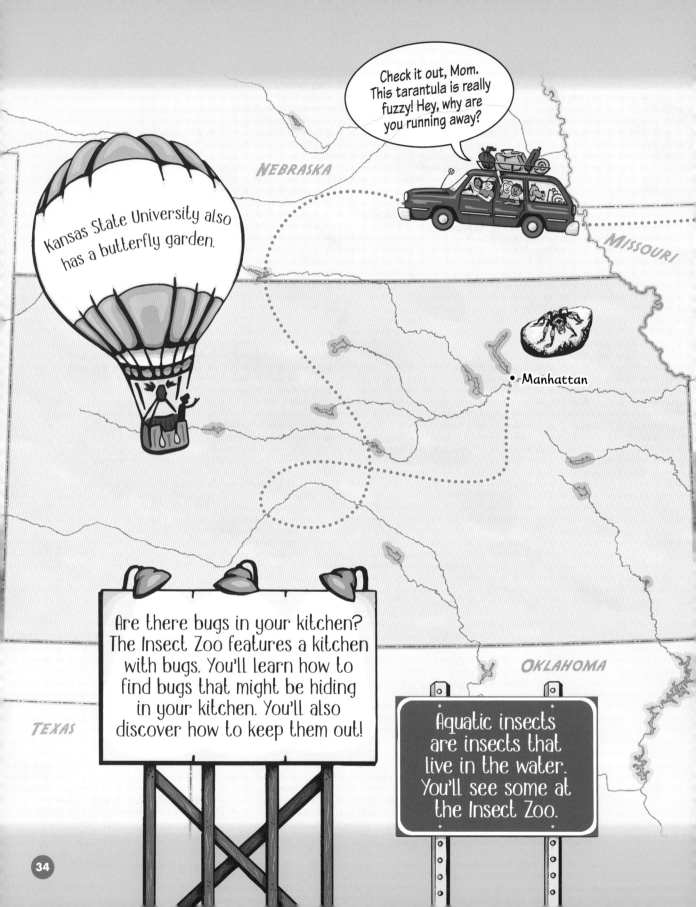

CREEPY-CRAWLIES AT THE INSECT ZOO

Would you like to pet a tarantula? Want a cockroach to crawl up your arm? Then stop by the Insect Zoo! It's at Kansas State University in Manhattan.

This is a great zoo for bug lovers. There's a lot of bug stuff to explore. One area is the bug petting zoo. You can hold and pet bugs there. Another area has a beehive. You'll watch the bees eating and even dancing!

One display keeps things dark. There you'll see what bugs do at night. It's all pretty amazing—if you like bugs!

See a beehive at the Insect Zoo!

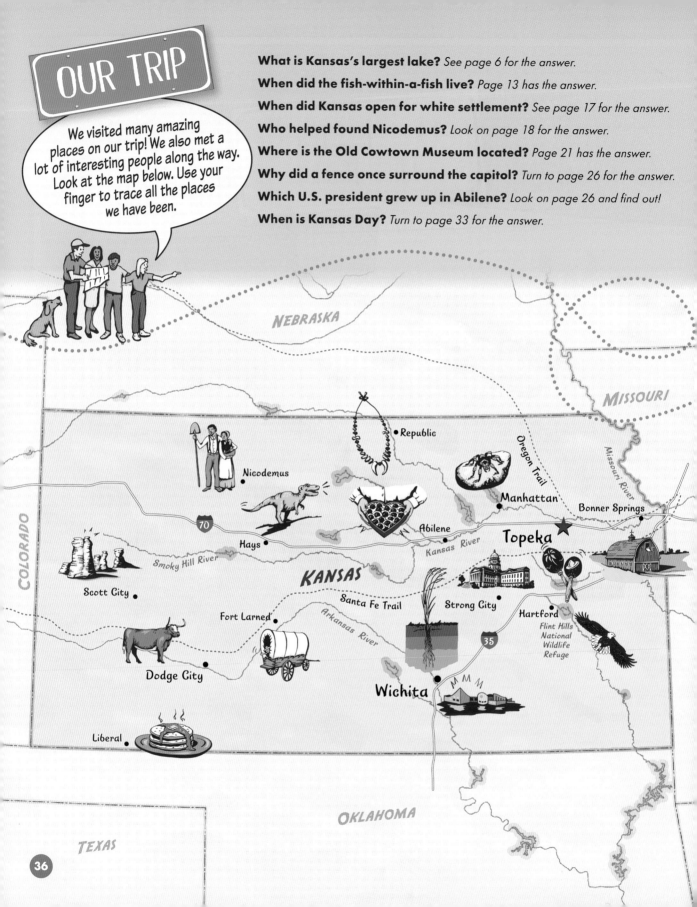

OUR TRIP

We visited many amazing places on our trip! We also met a lot of interesting people along the way. Look at the map below. Use your finger to trace all the places we have been.

What is Kansas's largest lake? *See page 6 for the answer.*

When did the fish-within-a-fish live? *Page 13 has the answer.*

When did Kansas open for white settlement? *See page 17 for the answer.*

Who helped found Nicodemus? *Look on page 18 for the answer.*

Where is the Old Cowtown Museum located? *Page 21 has the answer.*

Why did a fence once surround the capitol? *Turn to page 26 for the answer.*

Which U.S. president grew up in Abilene? *Look on page 26 and find out!*

When is Kansas Day? *Turn to page 33 for the answer.*

NEBRASKA

MISSOURI

Republic

Nicodemus

Oregon Trail

Manhattan

Missouri River

Bonner Springs

COLORADO

70

Hays

Abilene

Kansas River

Topeka

Smoky Hill River

KANSAS

Scott City

Santa Fe Trail

Strong City

Hartford

Fort Larned

Arkansas River

Flint Hills National Wildlife Refuge

35

Dodge City

Wichita

Liberal

OKLAHOMA

TEXAS

STATE SYMBOLS

State amphibian: Barred tiger salamander

State animal: American buffalo (bison)

State bird: Western meadowlark

State flower: Sunflower

State insect: Honeybee

State reptile: Ornate box turtle

State soil: Harney silt loam

State tree: Cottonwood

State seal

STATE SONG

"HOME ON THE RANGE"

Words by Dr. Brewster Higley, music by Daniel Kelly

Oh, give me a home where the buffalo roam,
Where the deer and the antelope play,
Where seldom is heard a discouraging word
And the sky is not clouded all day.

Chorus:
A home, a home where the deer and the antelope play,
Where seldom is heard a discouraging word
And the sky is not clouded all day.

Oh, give me a land where the bright diamond sand
Throws its light from the glittering stream
Where glideth along the graceful white swan,
Like the maid in her heavenly dreams.

Oh, give me the gale of the Solomon vale,
Where life streams with buoyancy flow;
On the banks of the Beaver, where seldom if ever
Any poisonous herbage doth grow.

How often at night, when the heavens were bright
With the light of the glittering stars,
Have I stood here amazed and asked as I gazed
If their glory exceeds that of ours.

I love the wild flowers in this bright land of ours;
I love too the wild curlew's shrill scream
The bluffs and white rocks and antelope flocks
That graze on the mountains so green.

The air is so pure and the breezes so fine,
The zephyrs so balmy and light,
I would not exchange my home here to range
Forever in azure so bright.

That was a great trip! We have traveled all over Kansas! There are a few places that we didn't have time for, though. Next time, we plan to visit the Eisenhower Presidential Center in Abilene. We can see the home of the 34th U.S. president! The Center also features a museum and library.

KANSAS

State flag

FAMOUS PEOPLE

Alley, Kirstie (1951–), actress, comedian, and spokesmodel

Bening, Annette (1958–), actress

Bosin, Blackbear (1921–1980), Kiowa-Comanche artist

Braungardt, Tanner (2000–), YouTube star

Brooks, Gwendolyn (1917–2000), poet

Chamberlain, Wilt (1936–1999), basketball player

Chrysler, Walter P. (1875–1940), automobile manufacturer

Dole, Bob (1923–), former senator

Earhart, Amelia (1897–1937), aviator

Earp, Wyatt (1848–1929), lawman

Eisenhower, Dwight D. (1890–1969), 34th U.S. president

Hopper, Dennis (1936–2010), actor

Hughes, Langston (1902–1967), poet and author

Inge, William (1913–1973), playwright

Johnson, Walter Perry (1887–1946), baseball player

Keaton, Buster (1895–1966), comedic actor

Kelly, Emmett (1898–1979), clown

Kenton, Stan (1911–1979), jazz musician

Lehrer, Jim (1934–), journalist

Martin, Bill, Jr. (1916–2004), children's author

McBride, Martina (1966–), singer, songwriter

McDaniel, Hattie (1895–1952), actor

Nelson, Jordy (1985–), American football player

Pitts, Zasu (1894–1963), actor

Sanders, Barry (1968–), football player

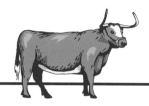

WORDS TO KNOW

descendants (di-SEND-uhnts) children, grandchildren, great-grandchildren, and so on

ethnic (ETH-nik) having to do with a person's race or nationality

fossil (FOSS-uhl) the hardened remains of a plant or animal

Hispanic (hiss-PAN-ik) relating to people with roots in Spanish-speaking lands

international (in-tur-NASH-uh-nuhl) involving more than one country

jalapeño (ha-la-PAY-nyoh) a very hot pepper

pioneers (pye-uh-NEERZ) the first European people to move into an unsettled region

TO LEARN MORE

IN THE LIBRARY

Ingram, Scott. *Kansas*. New York, NY: Children's Press, 2009.

Nault, Jennifer. *Kansas: The Sunflower State*. New York, NY: AV2 by Weigl, 2016.

Patent, Dorothy Hinshaw. *Camas & Sage: A Story of Bison Life on the Prairie*.
Missoula, MT: Mountain Press Publishing Company, 2015.

ON THE WEB

Visit our Web site for links about Kansas:

childsworld.com/links

*Note to Parents, Teachers, and Librarians: We routinely verify our Web links to make sure
they are safe and active sites. So encourage your readers to check them out!*

PLACES TO VISIT OR CONTACT

Kansas Office of Tourism and Travel

travelks.com
1000 SW Jackson St., Suite 100
Topeka, KS 66612
785/296-2009
For more information about traveling in Kansas

Kansas State Historical Society
kshs.org
6425 SW Sixth Avenue
Topeka, KS 66615
785/272-8681
For more information about the history of Kansas

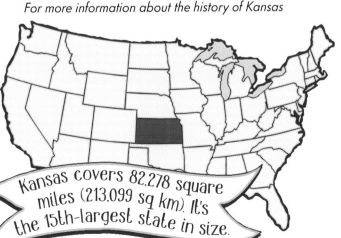

Kansas covers 82,278 square miles (213,099 sq km). It's the 15th-largest state in size.

INDEX

Bye, Sunflower State.
We had a great time.
We'll come back soon!